Here I Am

Kirsten LaMantia, Ph.D., LPC, NCC

Here I Am

Invincible Publishing
1714 Hampton Knoll Drive
Akron, Ohio 44313
T: (330) 923-8405
W: www.InvinciblePublishing.com
E: Info@InvinciblePublishing.com

Paperback ISBN: 978-0-692-67923-4
Library of Congress Control Number: 2016937544

Printed in the United States of America

Table of Contents

Dedication

To my Mom and Dad for their
constant love and support and
Holly for being my biggest
encouragement.

Acknowledgments

This play was first published as a hermeneutic phenomenological ethnodrama in my dissertation, *Voices of Minority Students Within Master's Level Counselor Training Programs*. Therefore, I want to thank my dissertation committee for helping me maintain a rigorous research process and approving a unique research methodology: Drs. Stephen Feit, Elizabeth Horn, Judith Crews, Alan Frantz, and Karen Appleby.

Secondly, I would like to express gratitude for Dr. Nicole Hill for your propelling mentorship and Dr. Lynn Bohecker for your incredible editing.

Finally, thank you to my ten participants. Without you, this book would have never been possible. Thank you for answering my call for participants and for

choosing to be open, honest, and
vulnerable with me throughout the
research process. I hope, if
nothing else, the outcome of this
research lets you know that *you
are not alone*.

Playwright's Note

The play is constructed from direct quotes from over 30 interviews exploring the experiences of ten self-identified minority counseling master's students.

Cast of Characters

GEE African American, male, late fifties.

YSERA White, non-binary transgender person, has a processing disorder, early twenties. Prefers 'they' and 'them' as pronouns.

MARY Latina, female, mid-twenties.

MATTHEW Native American, male, gay, early thirties.

MAE White, female, atheist, mid-twenties.

ROSE White, female, Buddhist, thirties.

BETH White, female, Mormon, thirties.

OLIVIA White, androgynous woman, lesbian, twenties.

AMY	White, female, attends a Historically Black College or University, thirties.
DAVE	White, male, in wheelchair, former college-athlete, late twenties. Can move head, neck, and has limited use of arms.

ACT ONE

SCENE I: Identity

SCENE OPENS WITH EACH CHARACTER IN THEIR OWN HOME SPACES, GOING ABOUT THEIR BUSINESS. ONE MIGHT BE MAKING TEA, GETTING HELP FROM A FRIEND, MEDITATING, GETTING READY FOR THE DAY, ETC. EACH ACTION REPRESENTS THE STORY BEING TOLD. LIGHTS FOCUS ON WHOEVER IS TALKING.

DAVE

I was on my way to the city, actually. And I went off the side of the road, flipped my parents' minivan. At the time, I was driving it. And I flipped it straight over the top, like twice. And

I flew up into the dash, dislocated my neck. It was… I don't know if I can draw my fists together, but it was totally displaced. My top vertebrae, my C4, went down in front of the C5, like this, and I was trapped with my head to the side in the back of the van. And in that vehicle I didn't like wearing my seat belt because, at the time, I was like 260 pounds because I had just gotten done playing football.

And let's see… Yeah, I wasn't wearing my seat belt because it made me all claustrophobic and stuff, and that's kind of what made me fly around in the vehicle. I got kind of lucky because I laid there for over an hour, almost two, listening to the cars drive by. And they couldn't see me because it was one of those little slight curves in the road and it was just a really remote country road. Highly traveled, but in a tough spot to see. Luckily a guy that was… I actually kind of like flipped up over his long country driveway… luckily he was pulling out to go to third shift. He saw something that just didn't look right because the van landed on its wheels. All the exterior lights went off so for all he knew, it was maybe two teenagers parking. But yeah, so he called it in to the deputy. Deputy comes out, just kind of poking around, didn't really expect to find much. He shined his light down in there, found me. And the crazy thing about it is, at that C4 level, you've got the breathing issues that start coming in.

Until… it was right when he got there that I

started getting labored breathing. But yet, two hours went by and I didn't have any issues. I was just really dazed, hit my head real hard. I had a big gash on my head. But the only other scratch on my body was a little gash on my knee. No broken bones. It was just… it was weird. So yeah, they airlifted me. Luckily it's only like a 20-minute airlift from where I was to the city, and I was at a top-notch hospital. The care was great there. Yeah, outstanding. And I'm trying to think… I feel like I've told this story so many times. I mean, it was traumatic but I wouldn't call it as traumatic as strength and conditioning for college football. So I popped up from it.

ROSE

We took a field trip my senior year of high school and we ended up going down south of here. We went there and there just happened to be a Buddhist priest if you will, a Rinpoche, giving a talk, and my instructor, who was Buddhist said, "Well, why don't we go? Let's see what it is."

We went and everything that he said was like, "This is why this happens. This is why that happens. Life is characterized by suffering and here is why - greed, ignorance, hatred, desire, and if you really think about it, if you analyze it, you see the truth in this," And the more I sat and listened to him and asked questions, the more I realized, "This is what I've been telling myself

all along," so it already
aligned with my own
belief system. Then I
took refuge in the
Buddhist practice. It's
called "taking refuge"
and you take refuge and
you proclaim yourself as
a Buddhist and I did that
maybe a day after.

Ever since then, it's
been a journey to
understand what that
means for me and I've
always been really
analytical. I've always
really been interested in
the mind and how it
works, so I'm interested
in neurology - not that I
understand it - but it's
there, all of that. It's
like the perfect storm
between Buddhist
philosophy and science
and psychology and it's a
very empirically-based
religion. I hate to call
it a religion, but it's
very scientifically-
minded, psychologically-
minded so it seems so

natural that where I am spiritually is where I want to be professionally. That's everything that led up to now...

GEE

I remember when there was a time I was in active addiction, I was doing coke on a regular basis and I was tired. I was asking God to give me a sign of what I should do, and I remember looking up in the sky for the lightning and all that stuff, this powerful message, and I ran a stop sign. I didn't know that was what the message was until later on, because I still kept falling down. I lost everything.

I didn't believe in God until I got into recovery. I went to treatment in September of 1996, and I reconnected with God on a beach in Boca Raton, Florida when there was a storm coming. The storm was so powerful; you could hardly walk against the wind. You know, the kind you have to turn your back for fear of being blown away, and you can see the storm across the ocean coming from Miami, and the lightning and all that stuff. The water was so high; I couldn't even see the sand. And we were just on the same beach the day before for meditation and they let us play in the sand on the beach. That's when I heard this voice talking to me, and I realized that voice always talked to me. I just never listened. So that's how I reconnected with God, and it's a God of my understanding, not anybody else's. I don't go to church or any of that stuff and I'm not, like, a religious zealot. Very seldom do I even talk about what I believe

because I don't need to.
It's just for me.

YSERA

This was two weeks ago.
My parents are like, "We
can pick you up and go
for dinner, we can pick
you up, go to the hotel
and drop our stuff off."
And I felt kind of
mischievous because I
picked the hotel option
so I can corner them at
the hotel but I didn't
mean it to be like a bad
thing. I just… that's the
place that I can get them
alone and then we can go
do something nice… if
they still want to even
go near me. So I was
like, "Okay, I have
something important to
tell you. It's been
pressing on me for a long
time." I was like, "I'm
transgender, "and they
were just like, "I don't
really know what that
means." I was like, "Oh,
God. I'm going to have a

lot of back tracking to do." So, they had a lot of questions, and my mom started crying and I felt kind of sick because I was like, "What does that mean? What are you crying about? Have I disappointed you completely?" It was overall good, anything where you are not being kicked out or your funding for school is taken away or you are disowned it's good to me. I was thinking about all my friends who rely on donations mostly because they are on the streets. I'm like that's not me… so it's good.

MATTHEW

I was born in the South Central US, raised there. My dad is full blood Cherokee he wasn't a big part of my life growing up. My mom is part Cherokee and she is very interested in sort of keeping those connections but at a distance. It wasn't until sort of later in life that she was like, "you know you're an Indian and you need to connect to that," and she ended up marrying another guy who was a full blood Choctaw. So a lot of that was sort of… what is my...what do I look like as a Cherokee kid in a Choctaw town? Because we lived in a town where everyone was Choctaw and so it was kind of interesting to create that sort of connection to the culture of being in a tribe, being connected. Everybody knows each other; everybody knows every one's business. It's very small and local, it's also very poor and so there are those connections of everyone does for everyone else, but also we don't really have a lot to go around and we don't really have a lot of expectations for ourselves. And I think that's even true for my parents. My parents never thought about a future per se, like if you got a job that didn't lay you off, like maybe that was as good as it gets. No idea what a career is or anything like that, and so that was sort of what I was raised in.

MAE

From a very young age I knew that there were different religions and different beliefs and so I kind of always wondered, "Why are there different interpretations?" So that was kind of always in the back of my mind. When I was five I stopped believing in Santa Claus and I was like, "Hmm. Magic doesn't exist anymore, so is religion really true?" That's when

I started first questioning it, when I was five years old.

Then, by the time I was 13, I started really digging into different religions. Between 12 and 13 I really started just diving into it and I became really interested in Islam. Oddly, I think it might have been because of 9/11. So I started really digging into that, and Judaism, and just all different kinds of stuff. I was just like, "There are so many different interpretations. They can't all be real." Everyone believes this, depending on what geographical location they grew up in and who their parents were, and so like if I was born in India, I might be Hindu. Also, when I was around the age of 13, I was just like... I never... I did look into Christianity and I

immediately discounted
that because I'd never
been taught, so that's
one thing, but then also
just the miracles, and
it's just all in magic
and superstition and I
just was like... I don't
know. Then when I was 14,
that's when I announced
that I was atheist to my
parents. They're not
happy about it, to say
the least, but they've
come to accept it.

BETH

I identify as Mormon or
LDS. A majority of the
community where my
program is are LDS. I was
not raised around here
though, like a lot of
people in my program are,
so there are things
about... sometimes I feel
like I get lumped into a
group of people when my
experiences within the
religious context are
different, so my way of
maybe expressing it, or

maybe even my thoughts on certain things are a little bit different, even though I've been given that label. I think it's commonly known with our religion, that our religion would say like, "homosexuality is a sin" so that might be like the religious doctrine of the church. I'm just going to be super open about it here but I might get emotional. My mom will be like:

                    CAST MEMBER

This person's bad because they're gay.

                       BETH

My mom will make comments like that and I'm like, "Mom, you don't even know that person. You don't even know anybody that's gay so how can you sit there and make judgments on who they are and what kind of person they are

just because of that?"
And I will say to her
things like, "We don't
know what they've been
through. We don't know
where they come from. We
don't know, what is their
choice, what is not their
choice. You don't know
anything about them or
their backgrounds so how
can you say that?" I
value my religion and I'm
not willing to just not
be a part of that. So
it's like grappling with
that a little bit. How do
I be in my religion that
I value and love and make
sense of this other stuff
and bring understanding
to other people?

OLIVIA

Being a gay person, it
wasn't always easy to be
so open and accepting of
who I was. So what people
think of as your "coming
out process," even though
you have to come out all
the time… There's not

just one coming out process. There's multiple, for the rest of your life, and a lot of people kind of forget about that. But the one that people are usually talking about, the one where it's like, "When you first realized you were gay, and you told your parents and all that stuff." When I think back to that time in my life and what I went through to get to a healthy place where I was accepting of me being a lesbian woman, and even harder accepting being an androgynous woman. That was even harder than accepting being gay, I think, to some degree. I couldn't accept that I liked masculine things until I accepted myself as a gay woman, and then I realized I wasn't alone. There were other butch androgynous lesbians out there, and this wasn't just a weird thing I do.

My mother and my father
have always been
supportive of me. It
wasn't easy when I first
came out. I'm not going
to say that. It took some
time for them to adjust,
but they were never like,
"This is a sin. You're
disgusting. You can't
bring anyone around." It
was never like that for
me. So I think knowing
that I had the love and
support of my parents
who... That's all any kid
ever wants, is the love
and support of their
parents. So it makes me a
lot more confident, and
that has definitely
helped me grow and
develop into the person I
am today. So now I'm not
scared. Internally, I
know. Yeah, people love
me and accept me for who
I am. Not everyone's
going to love me and
accept me for who I am,
but that's okay because I
have people who do.

MARY

I've always lived in very homogenous communities. I'm Mexican; I was born in the US but grew up in Mexico, a small, rural community kind of town. When I was 14, my mom ended up asking me if I wanted to go to the US to live with my relatives for a year, learn English, kind of polish everything, then go back home to Mexico. I was like, "Yeah, whatever." So, I left the country for a year. I thought it would be fun and exciting. We ended up all staying. And from being rooted in that Mexican culture and then, I guess, really being like the migrant experience, because for generations my family had been, like, coming and going, coming and going between the US and Mexico, like from my great grandparents time. We come, we leave and

then we come back, and
then we leave. A lot of
my classmates didn't see
their parents for years.
And I was fortunate, my
dad always has… he's a
legal resident so I could
see him more often, I
could see him maybe once
or twice a year. So, I'm
very rooted in that
Mexican migrant
experience, I guess. And
when I came to this city
and this neighborhood,
it's mostly Mexican-
American, Mexican. I went
to a small Catholic high
school and I grew up very
Catholic back home. And
in Catholic high school,
you need to read and
speak Spanish in order to
be kind of accepted into
the school because they
have a dual language
system. So it was all
like a 100% Mexican.

And then going to
college, I was the only…
one of the few Hispanic
girls in the school. And

that's where I had some
of my previous
experiences because I was
finally like in the big
community where I was
more of a minority where
I have to adapt to other
people's culture, or
another language, and
that's where I really
experienced the micro-
aggressions and blatant
racism from my peers,
from my professors, from
the administration. I was
put in a lower level
English class, even
though I was a straight A
English student in high
school. For some reason,
they thought because
English was my second
language, that I didn't
know how to speak
English, so instead of
being able to get my
English credit in one
semester, they made me
take two for a year.

AMY

Well it's my first semester. I've only had three classes so far, but I'm the only White person in my class. On my first day of class, once people started coming in it was just like, okay. Okay, I knew I was going to a traditionally Black school, but I just thought it would be a little more diverse. Even though I knew the tradition of this school I just ... I went to a state school for my undergrad and it was just every class was completely diverse and it's just a mixture of everybody. And so I was like, okay. I get embarrassed really easily, and I'm kind of shy, and I turn bright red and I'm like great, now it's even more noticeable that I'm going to be the shy embarrassed one and I felt like I just stuck out.

The only time the racial issue comes into play, I think it's more of me. Because especially with everything that's going on right now, I mean, you know my whole school does silent protests and things like that for the Ferguson cop and racial shootings and things like that. It's almost uncomfortable for me to go to class because I don't want to identify with being White. Like, it's hard being the only person, the singled out person. So, that's... I mean no one says anything. Everybody treats me as a friend and as an equal and everyone's super nice, but I don't know if it would be the same if I knew them outside of school. I don't know how we would all act.

SCENE II: Counseling Program

CHARACTERS' ENVIRONMENTS ARE NOW
REFLECTING SCHOOL, COUNSELING
SITES, AND PROFESSIONAL
ATMOSPHERE.

                ROSE

     I've always been really
     interested   in
     architecture,   in
     spiritual architecture,
     and spiritual art. I had
     just gotten done with an
     interview   at   another
     Christian-based
     university and I had just
     been accepted and I was
     like,   "There's   just
     something that doesn't
     feel quite right about
     it. I'm going to go give
     myself a self-tour at

this other university,"
and then it just snowed
and it's beautiful.

The architecture and the
churches and the chapels
and the snow falling and
the Christmas lights and
I was like, "It's
Hogwarts. You have to be
here." It was great. I
could just feel it
radiating in every beam
of the buildings and
every - the look on
people's faces as they
walked through campus and
even the crosses. These
are things that I used to
fight against when I was
younger and I used to be
like, "Oh, those
Christians, they're
screwy," or whatever. Now
that I'm getting older
I'm going, "You know
what? They're not screwy.
They're different. They
may believe in a
different system than I
do but that doesn't mean
that I can't connect with
them." I've been there

almost a year and there
has never been a doubt
that this is where I know
I need to be. Every day
there is something that
happens on a spiritual
level that tells me,
"This is it. This is
exactly where I need to
be, how I need to be
doing it."

MATTHEW

The second challenge
though is I know that I'm
gay and I know that I'm
out and I feel like
should I be the person to
say "hey what about the
gay kids"? And from human
development onward I feel
like in almost every
class, I've had to ask
myself, is it my
responsibility to be the
representative of the
minority in my class? And
I always sort of
challenge the class and
see if anybody else is
going to say anything.
Like, is somebody going

to mention gay kids? Or,
is the gay guy going to
mention gay kids or gay
clients? And so far, I'm
the only one who brings
it up. I feel...one,
that's good, because then
we are talking about it,
and it's a conversation
that happened in the
classroom. Two, it's a
little frustrating that I
have to bring it up. I
think that that has been
when I felt the most
marginalized I guess, and
it's interesting because
it is not harmful. I
don't feel threatened. I
feel disappointed, I
guess. Does that make
sense?

MAE

In my previous master's
program, I had to leave
there, actually, because
I had a conflict with a
professor who... He kind
of irked me when he would
start preaching in the
class. He came to the

39

university because it was a religious university, Lutheran, and he felt like he could be more open about his own beliefs in class and he announced that the very first day. Since then, he really talked a lot about Jesus and a lot about God. It was just really, really random and it made me feel really uncomfortable. I have a background in philosophy, in religious philosophy, because that's my other major in undergrad. Even then, no one ever preached to me or was trying to, I don't know, basically tell me the history of this person and just how I should use him in my counseling sessions to connect with clients and stuff like that. I was just like, this is not relevant at all to me because I'm never going to use Christian counseling, ever, and it wasn't a

Christian   counseling
class.

YSERA

I   call   myself   a   non-
binary   trans   person   and
as   far   as   I   know   in   my
program,   there's   no   one
else   that   identifies   like
that.   Sometimes   it   does
cause   some   trouble,
unfortunately,   it's   like
a   mis-gendering   kind   of
confusion   because   it's
not   like   trans   man,   or
trans   woman;   it's
something   in   the   middle.
Then   also,   I   do   have   a
few,   I   guess,
disabilities.   I'm   not
sure   if   that's   the
correct   word   but   I   do
suffer   from   PTSD   and
sometimes   that   causes
issues   within   the
program.   I   do   have   a
learning   disability;   it's
like   a   processing
disorder.

So,   I   posted   on   Facebook
this   kind   of   chart,   like,
when   is   it   okay   to   use

the R-word and of course
all going back to, "No,
it's not okay." Then this
person from my program
commented and said:

CAST MEMBER

This chart is retarded.

YSERA

They said the word and I
was like, "Oh." I tried
to inform him. I was
like, "That word does
hurt me," and then all my
friends came online that
have   learning
disabilities and they
were like, "That's never
okay to say," and then he
deleted it. He was like,
not   taking
responsibility. I sent a
message and I was like,
"I just wanted to say one
more time." He was like:

CAST MEMBER

It   was   meant   to   be
ironic.

YSERA

I was like, "I understand, but no," and then he deleted me from Facebook and I was like, "That's going to be fun for you; maybe we'll have to be partners in class sometime."

BETH

My supervisor at my site, she is very much like… I would say tries to be understanding of the LDS culture, is open to that, but also I felt like lots of comments that she would make were trying to let me know that my way of thinking was wrong. For example, I had a client that was gay and because maybe I'm not as familiar with that, I made a comment in one of my notes that said my client was LDS and my client said that because she chose a different lifestyle, her family didn't accept her. My supervisor assumed that I had made that comment, like it was by choice that she was gay, and I was making that assumption. It wasn't ill intended on my supervisor's part at all but I just would get undertones a lot of like:

CAST MEMBER

I wonder when people are going to realize that this is not a choice.

BETH

I felt like it wasn't like she was really making those comments. I think that's what she really believed but I felt like she was trying to educate me out of my religion and culture when that's already something that I feel, you know?

GEE

I had a bad experience in class with a peer. It was another adult learner in this class and I felt empathy for her because she was struggling with the here and now process. Because I like to help people and so forth, I kind of was trying to start a conversation with her. I started off the conversation by saying, "We're a lot alike." She's a White older lady. I'm Black, of course. And she looked at me with; I can't even describe the look. I just felt like she was looking down on me and she was like:

CAST MEMBER

We're nothing alike.

GEE

I was like, wow, before she even knew what I was really trying to say. And I'm like, "I'm so sorry," and I quickly walked away. But it really hurt me deeply. I had to actually process that with my support network to get through the feelings and the things that it brought up for me. So, when I came back to class, I am the kind of person that, she hurt me, I will leave you alone. I keep my distance and so forth.

It's like there are two people in me. There's one that grew up hard, that learned how to protect himself, that learned how to back people away and so forth through anger and so forth. And then this other part of me that wants to do the right thing and live the right way. But, I also have this third thing that's called, "my critical voice". It started running in my head and said:

ALL

You don't belong here.
You don't fit in. You
shouldn't be doing this.

OLIVIA

So my professor was
saying... I love my
professor. He's not
homophobic any bit at
all, and I just love him.
He's just so honest about
things and stuff, and he
said something like:

CAST MEMBER

I want to believe that
religious people can
believe in traditional
marriage and still be
accepting.

OLIVIA

So that just struck a
nerve with me because I'm
very passionate about
marriage equality. So I
raised my hand, and he
knew I was a lesbian
because he and I had

talked privately after class about something, and I outed myself to him. So, I raised my hand. I said, "I disagree with what you're saying. I think that religious people can be kind and nice to gay people and still believe in traditional marriage." I was like, "You cannot be accepting and denying people their basic human rights. You cannot say, 'I accept you, but I still find you different. So therefore, you're not allowed to have the same rights as me because you're different from me.' That's not being accepting. Others disagree with me, I'm sure, but I think that you can be a kind, loving person towards people, but that's not the same as being accepting." I said, "If you changed the word, I would agree with you. You can be nice to gay people and still be a religious person who believes in traditional marriage, but you cannot be a religious person who believes in traditional marriage and be accepting of gay people. The two just don't go together."

MARY

We were doing icebreakers and we wrote something on the paper. What was it? The professor handed out these papers, it was a sentence. You can't tell by looking at me but... and we filled it out. And I wrote something. You won't know by looking at me but I grew up in a very small rural community in Mexico, and the professor was like, "Oh, well, who might it be?" And one of my classmates was like:

CAST MEMBER

Oh, well, it's Mary. You would have the accent for it.

MARY

And looking back, that is not a big deal, it's not even an issue but I guess I was taken aback a little bit just because in my college experience, I was literally discriminated against by some of my college professors with comments like:

CAST MEMBER

Hispanics look alike.

CAST MEMBER

You can't speak Spanish in my class.

CAST MEMBER

Are you illegal?

MARY

Just very blatant comments in front of the classroom, in front of large groups of people that kind of made me a

little bit sensitive and
I'm like, "Really?" But
looking back at it, this
is not really an issue...
but sometimes I feel like
I'm a little bit... I don't
want to call it
oversensitive, but I tend
to react a little bit
more to comments like
that or little situations
that sometimes. I feel
like a micro-aggression.

THE SONG DRAMAMINE BY MODEST
MOUSE PLAYS

AMY

At the end of our class
last week or a couple of
weeks ago everybody had
to write down their
favorite song before we
left class, and for class
last week, our professor
played the song and we
had to guess everybody in
the class and who picked
which song. So, she went
through all the songs,
like two minutes of each
song, and we had to guess
who picked that song. And

then, like, advertisements would come on because she was playing Pandora, and it would be like a Beach Boys song in the advertisement and everybody looks at me. Just anything that wasn't hip-hop or R&B. I got guessed for like five different songs, because they wouldn't expect a Black person to pick something that would be a White song or something like that. I was like, okay. It draws a lot of unwanted attention. But it was just like, I guess for me, the entire thing, since it was 27 people, two minutes times 27, and the whole time I felt embarrassed. So it was just really hard to get through the entire thing. I was so happy when we had a break in the middle so I could re-group. Especially after the first two or three songs, I knew that everyone was looking for the different people because it would be the easiest to pick out. Not because they were picking on people, but that just is what made me feel so uncomfortable the entire time. And then, after class, everyone just joked about it.

MATTHEW

When I go back to my hometown is when my sort of native side comes out a little bit more, and my connections to my family, my brother and what not. If I'm in the last place I lived, where I have a lot of gay friends, my sort of gay side comes out. I feel "I'm turning the gay up; I'm turning the Indian up". Sometimes, in very few contexts, like maybe with one or two friends that I have who happen to also be Native and gay, where I feel this combination

is an interesting, unique
identity that we share
and experience, and so we
sort of talk and interact
in a different way. So I
think about that and I
put that into diversity
class, and I'm like, this
feels so awkward to...
Turn to the next chapter
where we are going to
talk about gay people;
the next chapter where we
talk about the disabled;
the next chapter we are
going to talk about Asian
Americans, and so on. And
then I don't know if
maybe that's the way it
was taught or the way
that specific book was,
but it felt inauthentic I
guess, sort of like a
zoo. Now moving on to the
next one, look at this,
ooh, ah!

MAE

I wrote up an official
complaint and I had
developed a petition. We
presented it to the

administrators and there
was this really big
investigation. The
teachers actually sat in
the class and listened to
him teach, and of course
when they sat in the
class, he didn't bring up
religion at all, unlike
all the other ones, so it
was not really
representative. So there
was a big thing.

After that, there was an
assignment where the
teacher created a fake
licensing board hearing
and she created different
scenarios for each
person. The scenario she
created for me was that I
had to pretend I was a
counselor who was
reported to the licensing
board hearing on charges
that I was demeaning
about someone else's
religion and that the
client felt that I
disregarded her religion
and tried to confront her
and tried to impose my

own beliefs. It wasn't just a regular assignment. That assignment was very, very hard for me because it made me feel like they actually thought that this was a possibility, that I could actually be brought to a licensing board hearing and have my counseling license revoked in the future because I wouldn't be able to deal with someone else's religion. Other people had scenarios that were like, "Oh, they received a gift from a client and they accepted it," or, "Oh, they had a sexual relationship with a client," or something like that. It wasn't anything related to something that they would actually do. Then when I had the licensing board hearing, it was three professors in the room, all three of them were that ones that were like… like one of them was the professor who preached the religion, so it felt like I was really on trial. I broke down, I just cried because it was just so intimidating. That was a really horrific experience for me, it was very traumatic. I wish it hadn't happened. I definitely think it was the main reason I decided to transfer.

DAVE

I love it. Everybody's awesome. Really, they are. You know, it was kind of funny, because the first day I roll into class in summer - our program goes summer, fall, spring, summer, fall, spring. I roll in this first day of summer classes and you know I'm kind of meeting people. I can kind of see it in some of the, you could tell the ones that were just fresh out of undergrad, at least from my perception. It seemed like they were kind of like, oh! They were kind of surprised. I just could tell that they hadn't seen too many people. I'm 6'5", like 230 right now. And my wheelchair is gargantuan. It was kind of funny to see their reactions to it.

But, they're all great people. Treated me just like anybody else. They come up; I live about 30 minutes away so I'm commuting down there. It's saved me a lot of money. But yeah, they come down here every once in a while. We go out to the movies and stuff because I've made friends, and I take advantage of my disability at times. I prey on people that pity me for some reason. [Laughs] At the movie theater, when it comes to buying tickets, Wednesdays and Sunday nights, this lady that works lets me in free. That, and handicapped placards, I'll never complain about, even though I don't even have to walk. But I do have an extreme sensitivity to cold... I'm always cold...

But yeah, as far as students go, I couldn't be happier. I think we got an awesome class. And I've heard that from our professors, too. We have a really unique, diverse class. There are 14 of us. And, I can't say enough about them, really, especially in the practice counseling. Everybody's really, really open. I think we're just that type of group.

END OF ACT I

INTERMISSION

ACT TWO

Scene I: Reflection and Expression

EACH PERSON IS REFLECTING ON
THEIR EXPERIENCES IN A SAFE SPACE
- HOME, CHURCH, COFFEE SHOP, ETC.

DAVE

So… since the last time
we talked, I did have an
experience… It's not
necessarily negative, but
it was something that was
a little, not irritating,
but it was just kind of a
letdown. It was basically
over spring break. A lot
of my classmates had been
able to get down to the
American Counseling
Association Conference. I
think I could've made

that happen had I known
ahead of time that many
of them were going. There
would've been a lot of
hoops to jump through,
and I'm still wondering
if it would've been
possible or not. That was
one thing. They almost
kept me out of the loop
on it and almost assumed
that that would've been
the case, that I wouldn't
have been able to make
it. I guess most of my
experience was positive
up to that point, and
then it gave me a
letdown. It was like, "Oh
shit." I think it's more
that they didn't know
what specific limitations
I had.

If they were more aware
in that realm, they
would've known that, hey,
this is doable. There was
a handful, some of the
students I probably hung
out with more, not that
there's too many cliques
evolving. I know of one.

He kind of knew that
there was a possibility
for sure, and I think the
outcome of this thing is
next year, I'm definitely
going to the next one.
But, I had no clue
anybody was going. It was
my first let down as far
as my disability
experience in my program.
It didn't bother me too
much. It was just sort of
a missed opportunity,
that drive to keep up and
prove myself like the
rest of them.

MARY

That makes me wonder
sometimes if it's me or
if it's also my
ethnicity. That one
starts coming in a little
bit more. It's just
people don't like this
specific Latina, like
this specific Latina
character, because I'm
not that stereotypical,
"Hey, Papi," that kind of
Latina, kind of like

Sofia Vergara character. Because I'm having these good relationships with people outside of the classroom who most of them happen to be Latino. But, other peers who are like, not Latino, and they're at my program, it's just not happening. So, maybe I'm not sure if it's because with my Latino friends we share the cultural background, we understand each other and why sometimes I have to go back home a little bit early because I live with my parents, and it's not that, with those friends who share the same cultural background.

AMY

Yes, it's making me think differently. I've always been pretty easy going to begin with, but I think more so now. The further I get into this program, it's kind of hard to be around a lot of other

White people. Like, it was hard to be around some White people to begin with, or just people in general to begin with, but just like you have friends that just say things without thinking, and now when they say things it's just like ... It's a little uncomfortable at first, but now you know you're really making me uncomfortable. You can't just say things; you're hurting people. It makes you look at diversity and all kinds of 'isms. I think it's even harder around family than around your friends, you know, because you're not going to change the ways of older people now. It's just uncomfortable and so if those conversations come up I redirect. I'm not even ... well, as you can see, I kind of do that a lot, but especially, I'm not going to start a fight with

that, have a big heated
discussion about race or
Obama or anything like
that just because you're
looking at one aspect of
the problem. And all
you're doing is looking
at the problem. You're
not trying to find any
solutions.

MAE

What happened at my old
school, it just really
made me question
everything that I was...
I really questioned even
continuing in this
program and stuff like
that, or like even being
a counselor because they
kind of made me feel also
that I wouldn't be able
to deal with someone who
was religious because I
couldn't deal with the
professor being religious
and stuff like that and
preaching in class. They
kind of told me:

CAST MEMBER

What if you get a
religious client? You're
not going to be able to
handle them.

MAE

I don't know. It just
made me really doubt
myself. Right now, I'm
going into an internship
that really bases its
whole program on
Alcoholics Anonymous, so
I'm learning more about
Alcoholics Anonymous
right now. There's that
fear again, that I'm not
going to be able to do it
because it has so much
about religion. It kind
of requires a belief in a
higher power in order to
see its effectiveness.
I'm just kind of worried
that I'm going to get
rejected or they're going
to find out that I'm an
atheist and I don't know.
It's like a fear that's

really been bugging me,
right?

GEE HOLDS A BOOK OF POETRY.

GEE

You know, I went to
treatment in 1996 and
poetry became my outlet,
a healing outlet for me
and I've been writing
ever since. It helped me
deal with a whole lot of
stuff that I probably
wouldn't have been able
to deal with without
writing. It became
therapeutic.
"Struggling", is one poem
that I wrote recently
because that's how I
felt, that I was
struggling because I
started my master's
program a week later than
everybody. It kind of
like is almost my life
story. The struggling
comes with fear, being
afraid of failing, being
afraid of not being good
enough, all those old
messages that I've

received throughout life from one experience or another. It was coming out as I started the graduate program, feeling like I wasn't good enough. It was a way of talking to myself and being able to reflect back on all of my experiences and realize that I came through a lot. T came through a lot of tough stuff and this is just another thing that I have to go through, that I can go through and excel at.

GEE PUTS ON READING GLASSES, READS POEM.

Struggling

It seems, at times, that life is always about struggling.

Two steps forward, one step back.

Internally, my own thoughts are what are befuddling.

It's me who I seem to want to attack.

Hindsight can be a painful dilemma of retrospection.

Useless waste of time, knowing I have other things to do.

Yet, I sit still allow my critic to do an inspection.

Then, I realize who I need to turn things over to.

The struggling lessens.

My thoughts are not my feelings.

I focus on the blessings.

I think of the process of healing.

The hurt child who was brought through a lot of heartache.

The opportunities I was gifted that helped me to turn around.

*Now, I have a decision to
make.*

*For what was once lost is
now found.*

*I am here for a reason
and my purpose is clear.*

*I am worthy of God's
love.*

*The valued friends and
family's love is what I
must hold dear.*

For many believe in me.

*So I am not struggling
anymore.*

*The solution is in my
spiritual clarity.*

*Look, there is another
door!*

YSERA

One of my textbooks
actually said something
terrible, "If you have a
mental disorder, should
you be a counselor?" And
I was like, "Probably
not." I literally said

that and I was like, "Oh,
that's a smack in the
face because the person
that writes the textbook
works in my program." And
I was like, "Mmm. I have
PTSD." I'm not always
feeling so wonderful, but
I don't really let it get
to me a lot. I deal with
stuff. At night, I have
nightmares and
flashbacks. I have some
issues but I feel like I
deal with them pretty
well.

When you asked for
pictures or poems, I was
like, "Hmm," because I
don't really make my own
art but I have my whole
PDF of poetry. It's
pretty dark and rough
stuff because some of it
is kind of old. It would
help you more hopefully,
maybe. That's not
anything recent so I'm
not depressed and scared
right now, but I have
some of my old stuff that
really is mostly about

trauma issues. I thought
it might help.

Organ Donor

*When I turned sixteen, my
license didn't have the
mark of an organ donor.*

*Back then, I saw my
organs as one of the few
things left as everything
was getting worse.*

*They kept me warm at
night.*

I was selfish.

*During the five years I
had to think about it; I
wanted to give them away
so bad.*

*The path to my uterus had
been marred by you, and
my brain stewed in your
callous remarks.*

*I would do anything to
change my status.*

I was selfish.

When I turned twenty-one, my license proudly displayed the mark.

My organs mean something now.

My heart can give love as fierce as a dam bursting, and my lungs breathe in pure air.

No longer selfish.

When I move on.

And all I can offer is that which is tangible.

I hope that you - whoever you are…

will take my organs, paint the night with them, kiss the trees, and love, just like me.

MATTHEW

I think that maybe this speaks to it, but when I started to do my internship, I ended up at the military trauma clinic in this city. I was a little nervous about that because I'm not a veteran and I'm going to be honest, there is some cultural homophobia that is present in the military. So again, it's another one of those negotiations; do I wear my wedding ring? How do I walk? What am I doing? How do I present myself? There are some things that I'm not... I'm too tired to change, I'm 30 years old. So, I'm not going to like deepen my voice, or start saying dude a lot more than I do, or use my hands less, or whatever I think might help. But, I do sort of go back to my skills, and I say all I can do is be here, and be open, and be warm, and this person is going to come in and set my dials, and then again the counseling session is going to be one those negotiations.

ROSE

So, I do have something
that felt like
discrimination since the
last time we talked. My
qualitative research
class instructor, she was
using a lot of God-based
readings to express
phenomenology. I felt
like that was very one-
sided and I would have
appreciated more accounts
of maybe people from an
atheist point of view,
like what would this be?
What would this look
like? We were doing a
unit on Eros and love in
one class. She said,
direct quote:

CAST MEMBER

Orgasming is like fucking
God.

ROSE

Direct quote, I swear. So
then I was like, well,
what if people are
offended by that? Maybe

some people are very Christian or very Catholic and they see that as a blasphemous thing to say, which I could certainly see.

Then I said, "Well, it's interesting that you bring that up, because in the Buddhist tradition, there are three times that you feel closest to God, and that's during death, enlightenment, and orgasm." She turns to me and said:

CAST MEMBER

You know, Rose, I'm not gonna go down the Buddhist road with you right now. If you want to take my spirituality class, it's available.

ROSE

I thought that I was really shut down by that, and that was the most powerful moment of that for me. I shut down, actually. I stopped participating as much. In some way, it was just if my voice is not allowed to be heard, then I might as well not speak at all. Who said this to me the first time? Somebody in college said to me, "Elementary school teachers love their students. High School teachers love their subjects. College professors love themselves." Have you ever heard of that? Yeah, and it's true. There is definitely a lot of ego, but not with everybody. Everybody else has been really wonderful. But, you get those select few that are just, why are you here? What is it within you that needs you to be defensive about being here?

BETH

I feel like sometimes I feel lonely. I feel like

I'm misunderstood. I feel
like people don't get it,
but yet I don't feel like
I can be vulnerable with
certain people and share
my experience of my
beliefs and why that's
important to me, why I
value it, how I see it or
look at it. Then I go to
church and there are
people that have some of
those negative things
that everyone's talking
about and I try to be the
person to… I feel like I
have to be the person to
stand up for people
outside the church, at
church, when stuff comes
up from people when
talking about this or
that. People who drink,
or people who smoke, or
people who swear, or
whatever it is. It's like
we all have our stuff, so
I'm defending people at
church, and I feel
isolated at church
sometimes, and then I
would go to my practicum
or school and feel like

I'm now defending my religious faith and who I am in those contexts. And I felt alone, like I don't fit anywhere. And I can be okay with allowing other people to make their own choices, and loving them, and respecting them, as long as they can love and respect me for my choices, too. And even if they don't, sometimes I'm going to love them anyway.

OLIVIA

Definitely when the LGBT Community is brought up, it's more like I wake up. If I'm getting tired in class, I'm like, "Oh, we're talking about LGBT things." So, I definitely pay more attention. I'm more in-tune. It's definitely like… I don't know how… my body language changes. I'm thinking a lot more than I usually am, especially

because there's this
feeling, too, of when I
speak as a gay woman, I'm
speaking for every gay
person out there, even
though it shouldn't be
that way, but
unfortunately, that's how
it comes across. It's
like:

CAST MEMBER

Well, I had a gay
classmate who said this.
So therefore, it applies
to all gay people.

OLIVIA

So that's a lot of
pressure. I need to
present myself in a way
that is responsible and
makes the community look
good. Because if I say
something that's
unintelligent, or not
politically correct, or
not up to date, that's a
reflection not only on
me, but on the community.
That's also hard too. So,

my body language will
change.

Then you have to play
this game of, "Okay. Do
you speak up now? Do you
not speak up? And how
much do you say?" Because
you don't want people
just to tune you out
because you're saying all
these great things about
the community, and
they're just like:

CAST MEMBER

Oh, I'm never going to
get it.

OLIVIA

You have to know how far
you can push the
conversation. I think
that kind of gives a good
picture of the way that
you address the situation
in a class and the things
that go through your mind
and stuff like that.

MARY

I do agree that part of
it is a little bit of
feeling lonely. It's a
different kind of lonely,
where you are in a room
full of people that you
see on a weekly basis,
even a few times a week,
but somehow you're
sitting next to 25 other
individuals, but you feel
that loneliness of not
being able to reach out
to them, or them not
responding to you
reaching out to them.

Scene II: Coping

BETH

This is what I try to remember when I am feeling different from others, lonely in my circumstances, or isolated in some way.

BETH TAKES OUT PAPER, BEGINS TO READ.

Unity in Diversity by Elder John K. Carmack, March 1991

We each need to assign ourselves as a "committee of one" to create the attitudes of inclusion, acceptance, and unity wherever we find ourselves. It needs to be a high priority with us.

We especially need leaders to show the way by precept and example. Each of us should be fair to everyone, especially the victims of discrimination, isolation, and exclusion. Let us be careful not to snicker at jokes that demean and belittle others because of religious, cultural, racial, national, or gender differences. All are alike unto God. We should walk away or face up to the problem when confronted with these common and unworthy practices. Each should do his or her part.

MAE

I actually found a client who was atheist, also. I really connected with him and he really made me think about what the higher power was and how that would impact someone who's going through an AA

program who doesn't
believe in God, how their
beliefs might prevent
them from moving on. I
connected with him on
that level. And no one
else could. My supervisor
doesn't understand it. It
was basically just me.
And I've since been his
individual counselor
because of the fact that
I related so well with
him.

And, I went above and out
of my way for him, a
little bit. I started
reading this book called,
Waiting: A Nonbeliever's
Higher Power. And I got
quotes from that and I
wrote them all down
because he's been really
struggling with the
fourth step. And so, I'm
going to give him that
when he comes in. And I
found that really
interesting that just
that tiny little bit,
even though we have
nothing else in common,

but that tiny little thing about being a minority and believing in science rather than faith kind of connected us. So, that was cool. That was really cool.

GEE

I don't have an African American role model to go to and say, "Hey I'm struggling with...", you know, baggage. I don't have a professor I can go to that I feel would understand. When I write, I still write kind of like how I talk, I say *is* instead of *are*. I had a professor that is really kind of hard, in a good way. He doesn't accept less than his standards. He seems vested in helping me to improve and to learn and to apply what I am learning. I'm supposed to meet with him in about 15 days and he wants to sit down and talk with me about

different things that I
can do better and help me
focus and so forth. I
guess it was from my
final paper that I wrote
and his critique of my
final paper. I would
imagine that he has
encountered many people
like myself and sees
potential possibly.
That's what I take out of
it. At first, I had a lot
of fear and I'm thinking
of those old messages
playing in my head. And
you know, and part of it
is it ties into the
authenticity. It's like
part of me is afraid that
I'll start talking
differently and become a
different person because
I need to speak properly,
you know, which is just
kind of silly but it's
fear based. But, I'm
looking at it positively
now. He is vested in
helping people. That is
why he is doing what he
is doing. I am just going

to go into that meeting
with an open mind.

OLIVIA

Even though I am
comfortable with myself,
you still have that
little bit of an
adrenaline rush right
before you actually come
out to people, especially
like that time with the
professor when I
vocalized my opinion
about traditional
marriage and religious
people. My heart was
definitely like,
"[noise]," because I'm in
front of the whole class.
Literally, I'm in front
of the whole class
because I sit in the
front of the room, and
metaphorically, in front
of the whole class.

So, that's definitely
something that I don't
think will ever go away,
regardless, in school, or
just in life. You're
always going to have that

little bit of an adrenaline rush right before you come out to someone. And, like I said, because I am androgynous, most people usually jump to conclusions that I am a lesbian, just based off of the way I dress, and how I present myself, and those types of things.

But, when I actually have to vocalize it, that's definitely a little bit of a wake-up. It's like, "Okay. I'm going to say this." You don't know how someone's going to react. Most of the time, it's positive, but the times when it's negative, that kind of sticks with you a little bit more, unfortunately. So, you do kind of do a little bit of pep talk inside, and you get a little bit of an adrenaline rush… and then you do it. You come out.

MATTHEW

It is sort comforting to know other people who feel like they're, "the other", in the room are also debating like, "When do I say anything at all?" and, "How do I even say it so I don't sound like the voice on the mountain?" Sometimes, I wonder, do other students have this issue? In some ways, it's interesting. I wonder if they perceive their statements as, "me", as an individual that feels this way. But, then when I speak, am I talking for men, am I talking for gay guys, am I talking for people of color? You almost want to ask, "Who do you think I'm speaking for right now?"

MARY

I've noticed a couple very, very, very, very subtle changes with my classmates, maybe two in particular, that say, "Hi", every time I come into the classroom now, which I found odd, but I think it's because I helped one of them. I told her that one of the books for the class that's pretty expensive is online for free in the library. I think she appreciated that, so now she's like, "Hi", every time I walk in. I'm like, "Me?" That one subtle change. I did a presentation and people said, "Oh, good job, Mary", and I'm like, "Thank you". So, it's been a few instances like that. I'm like… hmm, I'm not sure how to handle this. [laughs] It's been nice.

I'm kind of resigned to the fact that I might not make these friendships and great relationships with people, but I'm okay with it. I'm comfortable

with who I am. I have
great relationships
outside of that program,
and it's not something
new, these feelings. It's
something that I can cope
with that's not making me
depressed. I think in the
beginning it was so new
and I was so hopeful,
like, oh, a graduate
program. I was like, make
these great connections
and kind of stay in touch
with these people after
my program and it's going
to be great. Now that I'm
finishing my first year,
and I reflect more about
it, it's like I'm okay
with it. If it continues
like this, it's not very
fun, but I do what I have
to do.

MAE READS FROM A PIECE OF PAPER.

MAE

*Waiting: A Non-Believer's
Higher Power By Marya
Hornbacher*

Call it the feeling of love that connects us. Call it the creative force that drives us to transform. Call it our energy. Call it our capacity to give. Call it grace, or even divinity, something that allows for those things to exist within us as individuals and between us each time we connect. Call it the forces of good and evil, love and hatred, creative and destructive energy, wonder and awe, pain and suffering – while I contain all of these things, while all humans do, their cumulative force in the larger world is more powerful than I am myself. We are not asked to understand this power, we are only asked to believe that we can be healed by these myriad forces that surround us and that we possess.

ROSE

For the first time, I
felt lonely in my
program. Did you ever see
the movie, *Contact*? I
remember the opening
scene when that movie
came out, how loud our
planet is and how you had
to get so far. Then it
started with the
television, and then it
panned out further and
further and further into
the atmosphere, and then
further and further and
further into the
Satellite field, and then
past that into... between
the Earth and the Moon,
and then past that, and
it took so long. It took...
if we were to have taken
a ship from Earth to past
Pluto, that's how long it
would have taken for the
sound to just abate. Even

then you could still hear
broadcast from the 1930s…
That really made me think
how loud everything is,
and how can you possibly
think when there's so
much noise all the time.
There really is so much
noise.

I feel like that ties
into self-care where
there is just so much
sound, and there's not
enough quiet… Since the
last time we talked, my
husband and I went into
the desert. I love the
desert. It was so
refreshing for me to be
able to open a door and
there was nothing. It was
just the stars, and there
was a meteor shower, and
the coyotes howling, and
everything was so
beautifully… nothing. I
mean, it was vivid and
real, but it was empty of
extraneous concerns.

It was like, it made me
so present. And at first,
I felt this fear like,

"Well, where is my noise?
Where is it?" And then I
realized, but this is my
heart, this is my home,
this is everything, and
how can I feel alone when
I am here? And I didn't.

AMY

We went to have drinks
after our last class.
Everybody got together at
a restaurant down the
street. So, one of the
girls that I'm a little
bit closer to, she was
like, "Oh, I've got my
weave in today." And all
the other girls were
excited. I looked at her
and I was like, "I just
don't understand." This
is something a little bit
lighthearted but I still
don't know anything about
it and these are my
cohorts. Then, they were
explaining some things to
me, and then one of the
other girls that I'm not
as close to, but she's
going to be in my

graduating class and
everything, she looked at
me and she was like:

CAST MEMBER

You know what? I really
appreciate it that you
just admitted that and
asked how it works. Even
though it's something so
simple. There's this
Caucasian woman I work
with and she came up to
me, touched my hair and
came into my personal
space. And instead, you
just asked and said, "I
don't know what you're
talking about", instead
of invading my space.

AMY

So, that helps me realize
that even though it's
different, I can just
ask. I can just be frank.
I don't know if that's as
easy for other people to
do or feel comfortable
with. But, by taking one
little step like that,
I'm like, "Okay, so I

could go a little bit
further." And, I think
that also helps them to
realize that I'm just
curious. I don't know.
I'm just curious and, you
know, it's just different
for me.

DAVE

But yeah, I guess I never
realized I was really
nervous going into a
Master's program, about
my abilities in a
classroom, and just
writing papers in
general. Yeah, I had
always been okay at
writing, you know,
talking. Whatever. I
could talk in front of
some people, that's fine,
but surprised, yeah, a
little bit. I just got
put on a scholarship for
getting really good
grades. I've only gotten
one B so far, I think. I
was surprised at that.

As far as classroom
accommodations, and the

curriculum, and the academic experience, they've been awesome, really, really good. Was I worried about it, about learning what resources were there and how to use them? I had no idea about working with SDS services, about the school part of it, or how the class attendant type stuff was going to go - didn't know. It ended up being a lot simpler than I thought. You take it all into consideration, like I said, adaptability.

YSERA IS THE FIRST PERSON TO BEGIN TO SPEAK WITH/TO THE OTHER CHARACTERS.

                    YSERA

It felt nice to know that even though we're all across America, I guess, that we share a common thing. Maybe that's how all of us feel even if we're not minorities, like everyone probably feels like, you know, where is my place in this? But there is a place for everyone. And, it's nice to see that - that you can kind of get through it by just giving it a chance, and expressing yourself, and just being... I think being authentic is really important, just being upfront. Because I know how much it hurts to just hide and hide. And I also know that sometimes it is necessary. I think you feel much better if you just like put it out there. And then they can accept you or not. But really, it's not your responsibility if they like you or not. You just have to keep going. Because I'm learning that the program is tough. It's not what I thought it would be. But, I'm kind of glad that it isn't what I thought. It challenges you to really get out of your comfort

zone and be vulnerable.
That's what I've been.
Now I'm just taking risks
left and right. It's
like, you know, answer
this question in class.
And I'm not questioning
if what I have to say is
worth it or not. You
know, it's just like,
here I am.

Scene III: Wisdom

CHARACTERS ARE IN A LINE,
SPEAKING DIRECTLY TO THE
AUDIENCE.

                ROSE

    The   individuals   that
identify   with   minority
groups - I think really
the best thing they can
do   is   work   on   being
resilient, because like I
said, there is going to
be people everywhere that
are going to be horrible,
and people that are going
to say things, and people
that   are   going   to   do
things. I guess I would
say   the   first   thought
that comes to mind is I

want to pump them up and
get them like, "Yeah, you
can do it. Don't worry
about it. You're worthy.
You can do it. You're
smart. You're good
enough. You're smart
enough. People like you!"

OLIVIA

My advice would be to
love and accept yourself,
as hard as that is, but
you're not going to get
love and acceptance from
anyone else until you
love and accept yourself.

MATTHEW

If you feel like you are
the other, you are the
other, there are going to
be opportunities that
come from that if not for
your entire class, then
at least for yourself. I
have taken the time to
reframe it as: I'm
learning a lot about
White women. That's
another thing that I've
got going for me from

going through the program. I think that it's been okay. I would encourage them to always fill out the feedback form and mention that there's a lack of diversity in their class.

MARY

I would say make an effort to get to know your classmates. They're all going to be great contacts later on in the future, even if it's a little bit hard, try to reach out to people. Talk, mingle, and attend the events as much as you can, reach out to your professors if you see something's not working out. Reach out for help, because even if you don't think it's going to help, there might be someone else. Your professor can connect you with someone else that can give you advice that you didn't think about before.

MAE

Reach out to people, whether it's through the internet or through some kind of group of people that you have something in common with.

DAVE

I'd probably try to empower the shit out of them. [Laughs] You know, that's kind of my go-to. I'm a big one on, where there's a will, there's a way - encouragement, empowerment, and resources. I'm a big one on tapping into resources and advocating.

BETH

I would say and I've thought about this before. I would say we all have reasons why we are different. But we are so focused sometimes on our differences, or the thing that makes us different, and how we

don't fit, that it keeps
us from being open to
other people. Value the
differences that you have
because you have a
different perspective to
offer people, and be
willing to be
understanding of other
people's differences too.

AMY

I would say just be, and
I should take my own
advice probably, but just
being confident in who
you are. Like everybody's
there to learn from each
other and you don't have
to be like everybody
else. That's what makes
for a better learning
experience. You know you
should appreciate the
fact that you're
different and embrace it.
Because, I mean, it
causes a lot of
conversations if you're
willing to be in them,
and a lot of debates, and
room for growth.

GEE

One of the things that I
would tell them is to
surround themselves with
strong peer support - to
get a network, and start
now to build a network
that you can use in the
future.

YSERA

I don't know you... but who
you are is so special and
other people can't
understand that now, but
in the future they will.
And whoever you choose to
counsel, they will see
that in you, that you do
have skills, and just
because you might be from
a different part of life,
or there is something
different about you, you
have been through a lot,
so you do have the wisdom
and the knowledge, and
you've fought through so
much that if you could
just... you get your

degree and then you help others.

END OF PLAY

Discussion Questions

1.) What is/was your experience like as a master's counseling student? Was there anything that differentiated you from your peers? Were there times you felt lonely?

2.) What were your reactions to each character? Were there some with whom you identified? Were there any about whom you felt strongly?

3.) How did the characters change or grow as the play progressed?

4.) What themes did you see as consistent throughout the play?

5.) Were there any cultural concerns you had not considered?

6.) After reading this play, how might you work differently with peers, students, or clients in the future?

7.) The last scene of the play is advice the characters would give other self-identified minorities. Based on your own lived experience, what advice would you give to people in a similar situation as yours?

About the Author

Kirsten LaMantia, Ph.D., LPC, NCC, is an assistant professor in the Department of Educational Leadership and Counseling at Southeast Missouri State University in Cape Girardeau, MO. She graduated with a BFA in Acting from the Chicago College of Performing Arts at Roosevelt University in Chicago, IL, an MA in Community Counseling from Saint Xavier University in Chicago, IL, and a PhD in Counselor Education and Counseling from Idaho State University in Pocatello, ID.

Her counseling expertise includes individual and group counseling for victims and child witnesses of domestic violence. She has presented nationally and internationally on topics such as feminist theory, LGBTQ+ populations, and multicultural competence within counselor education and counseling.

CPSIA information can be obtained
at www.ICGtesting.com
Printed in the USA
LVOW12s2001150916

504784LV00018B/321/P